**Title:**

Crypto Cashout: Simple Strategies for Profiting from Cryptocurrency on Your Phone

Maxwell Cowell

Maxwell Cowell

# Chapter 1.  Introduction:

Welcome to "Crypto Cashout: Simple Strategies for Profiting from Cryptocurrency on Your Phone." In this book, we'll explore the exciting world of cryptocurrency and provide you with practical strategies to cash out your digital assets using just your smartphone.

Cryptocurrency has revolutionized the way we think about money and investing, offering unprecedented opportunities for financial growth. However, navigating the complexities of the crypto market can be daunting, especially when it comes to cashing out your investments.

Whether you're a seasoned investor or just starting out, this book is designed to demystify the process of cashing out cryptocurrency. We'll cover everything from choosing the right exchange and setting up your mobile wallet to understanding security measures and managing fees.

By the end of this book, you'll have the knowledge and confidence to effectively cash out your cryptocurrency holdings, maximize your returns, and achieve your financial goals. Let's embark on this journey together and unlock the potential of crypto cashouts right from the palm of your hand

Maxwell Cowell

# Chapter 2. Understanding Cryptocurrency and Its Market:

Cryptocurrency, often referred to simply as "crypto," is a digital or virtual form of currency that utilizes cryptography for security and operates on decentralized networks based on blockchain technology. Unlike traditional currencies issued by governments and central banks, cryptocurrencies are typically not controlled by any single entity, making them immune to government interference and manipulation.

At the heart of cryptocurrency is the blockchain, a distributed ledger that records all transactions across a network of computers. This technology ensures transparency, immutability, and security, as each transaction is verified and recorded by multiple participants in the network.

The cryptocurrency market is dynamic and constantly evolving, with thousands of different cryptocurrencies available for trading. Bitcoin, created in 2009 by an unknown person or group of people using the pseudonym Satoshi Nakamoto, is the first and most well-known cryptocurrency. Since then, numerous alternative cryptocurrencies, often referred to as "altcoins," have been created, each with its own unique features and use cases.

The cryptocurrency market operates 24/7, allowing users to trade digital assets at any time of day or night. Prices can be highly volatile, with dramatic fluctuations occurring within short periods. Factors influencing cryptocurrency prices include market demand, investor sentiment, technological developments, regulatory news, and macroeconomic trends.

Understanding the fundamentals of cryptocurrency, including blockchain technology, market dynamics, and price movements, is essential for successful investing and trading. In the following chapters, we'll delve deeper into these topics and explore strategies for navigating the cryptocurrency market effectively.

# Chapter 3. Choosing the Right Exchange for Your Needs:

Selecting the right cryptocurrency exchange is crucial for your trading and cashing out experience. With numerous exchanges available, each offering different features, security measures, fees, and supported assets, it's essential to consider several factors before making your decision.

**Security**: Security should be a top priority when choosing a cryptocurrency exchange. Look for exchanges that implement robust security measures such as two-factor authentication (2FA), cold storage for funds, encryption protocols, and regular security audits. Additionally, check the exchange's track record for handling security incidents and how they communicate with users in case of any security breaches.

**Reputation** and Reliability: Research the reputation and reliability of the exchange within the cryptocurrency community. Look for reviews, user feedback, and any past incidents or controversies involving the exchange. Choose exchanges with a proven track record of reliability, uptime, and transparent operations.

**Supported Assets**: Consider the range of cryptocurrencies supported by the exchange. While most exchanges offer popular cryptocurrencies like

Bitcoin (BTC) and Ethereum (ETH), some may have a more extensive selection of altcoins. Ensure that the exchange supports the cryptocurrencies you intend to trade or cash out.

**Trading Fees:** Exchanges typically charge fees for trading, depositing, withdrawing, and other services. Compare the fee structures of different exchanges and consider how they may impact your trading profitability. Look for exchanges with competitive fees and transparent fee schedules to avoid unexpected costs.

**User Interface and Experience**: The user interface and experience of the exchange can significantly impact your trading experience, especially if you're new to cryptocurrency trading. Choose exchanges with intuitive, user-friendly interfaces,

comprehensive charting tools, and responsive

customer support to streamline your trading

experience.

**Liquidity**: Liquidity refers to the ease with which

assets can be bought or sold on an exchange without

significantly impacting the market price. Higher

liquidity ensures faster execution of trades and

tighter bid-ask spreads. Research the liquidity of the

exchange's markets, particularly for the

cryptocurrencies you plan to trade.

**Regulatory Compliance**: Ensure that the exchange

complies with relevant regulations and has

appropriate licenses and registrations in jurisdictions

where it operates. Exchanges that prioritize

regulatory compliance are more likely to offer enhanced security measures, investor protection, and transparent operations.

**Customer Support:** Consider the quality and responsiveness of the exchange's customer support services. Look for exchanges that provide multiple channels of communication, timely responses to user inquiries, and comprehensive support documentation to assist users with any issues or questions.

By carefully evaluating these factors and conducting thorough research, you can choose the right cryptocurrency exchange that aligns with your trading preferences, security requirements, and overall needs. Remember to start with small trades and gradually increase your exposure as you become more familiar with the exchange's features and

functionality.

# Chapter 4: Introduction to the DEFVR Strategy

The DEFVR strategy, which stands for Divergence EMA, FVG (Force Volume Graph), Volume, and RSI (Relative Strength Index), is a comprehensive trading strategy that integrates multiple technical indicators to identify potential trend reversals and trade opportunities in the cryptocurrency market. By analyzing divergence between price and the Exponential Moving Average (EMA), along with Force Volume Graph (FVG), volume, and RSI, the DEFVR strategy aims to capture shifts in market sentiment and momentum with added confirmation from RSI signals.

**Parameters of the DEFVR Strategy:**

**Divergence EMA:** Divergence between price and the Exponential Moving Average (EMA) is a key component of the DEFVR strategy. EMA is a type of moving average that gives more weight to recent price data, making it responsive to short-term price movements. Traders look for divergence between price and EMA, where the price is making new highs or lows but the EMA fails to confirm the same trend. Bullish divergence occurs when price makes lower lows, but the EMA makes higher lows,

indicating potential bullish reversal.

Conversely, bearish divergence occurs when price

makes higher highs, but the EMA makes lower lows

, signaling potential bearish reversal.

Picture 1.

Maxwell Cowell

Price was ranging while EMA was going bearish.

That is Divergence.

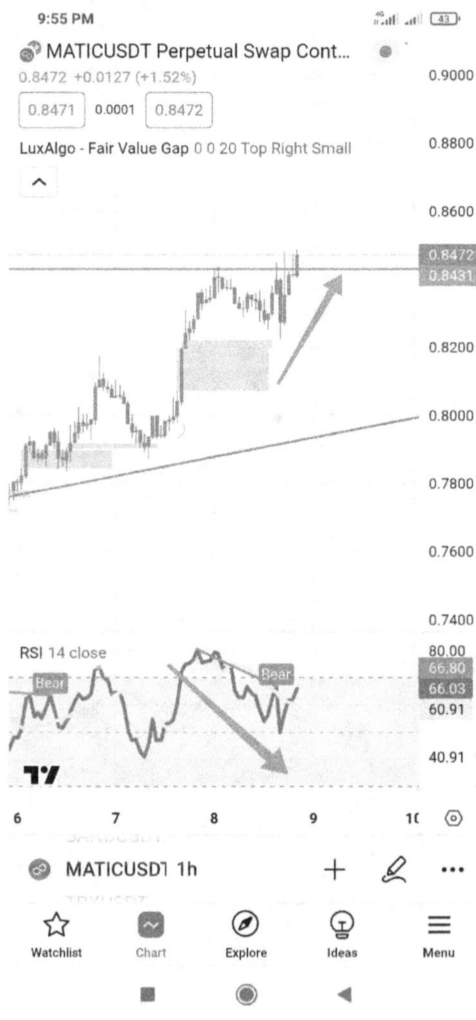


Maxwell Cowell

# Picture 2.

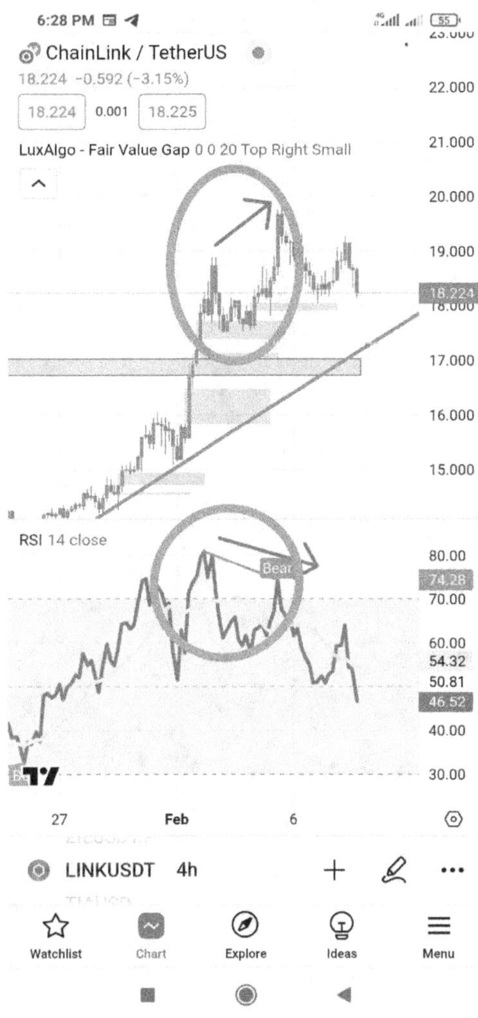

# Picture 3.

Maxwell Cowell

Picture 4.

Maxwell Cowell

**Force Volume Graph (FVG): The** Force Volume Graph (FVG) is a technical indicator that combines price and volume data to measure the strength of buying or selling pressure in the market. It plots volume bars along with price movement, allowing traders to visualize the relationship between volume and price changes. High volume accompanied by price movement in the same direction indicates strong market conviction, while divergence between volume and price may signal a weakening trend or potential reversal.

Picture 5. Positive FVG

Negative FVG automatically plotted .

**Volume**: Volume refers to the total number of shares or contracts traded in a given period. In the context of the DEFVR strategy, volume analysis helps confirm the validity of price movements and divergence signals. Increasing volume during price advances or declines suggests strong market participation and validates the current trend. On the other hand, decreasing volume during price movements may indicate weakening momentum and potential trend reversal.

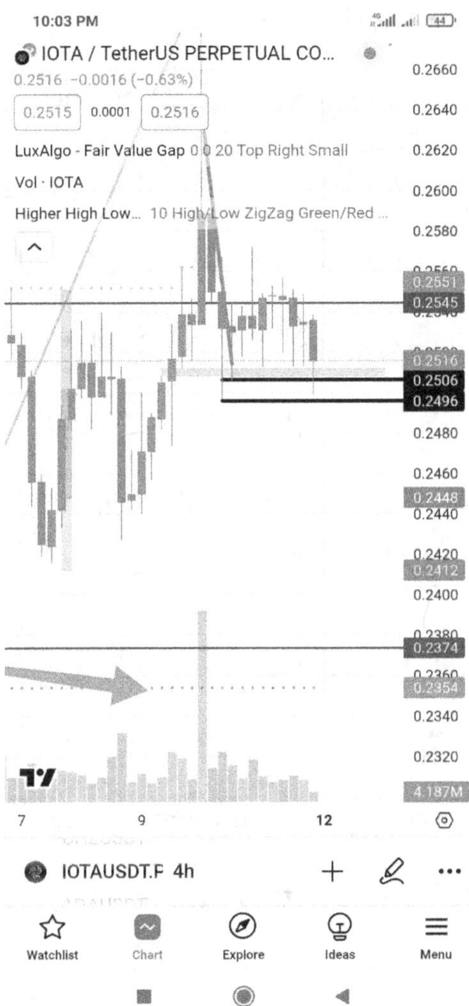


Picture 6.

Maxwell Cowell

**RSI (Relative Strength Index):** RSI is a momentum oscillator that measures the speed and change of price movements. It oscillates between 0 and 100 and is typically used to identify overbought or oversold conditions in the market. In the context of the DEFVR strategy, traders use RSI to confirm divergence signals and assess the strength of price movements. A high RSI reading (above 70) suggests overbought conditions, while a low RSI reading (below 30) indicates oversold conditions. Divergence between RSI and price movements can also provide valuable insights into potential trend reversals.

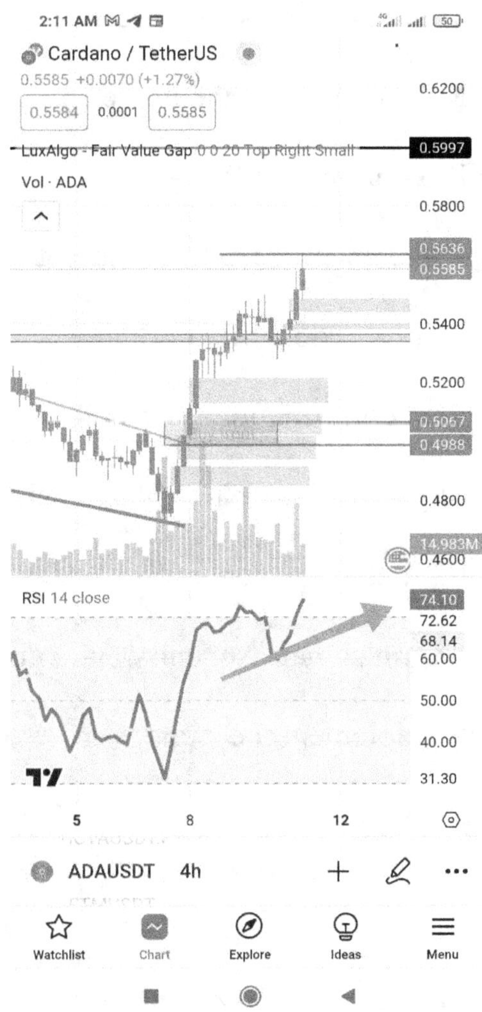


Picture 7.

Maxwell Cowell

By integrating these four parameters – divergence between price and EMA, analysis of the Force Volume Graph (FVG), volume, and RSI – traders can gain a comprehensive understanding of market dynamics and identify high-probability trading opportunities with added confirmation from RSI signals. In the following sections, we'll explore each parameter of the DEFVR strategy in detail, discussing how to interpret signals, set entry and exit points, and effectively implement the strategy in real-world trading scenarios.

# Chapter 5: Step-by-Step Guide to Cashing Out on Your Phone

**Choosing a Cryptocurrency Exchange Company:**
Before you can cash out your cryptocurrency on your phone, you need to choose a reliable exchange platform. Popular options include Binance, OKEx, Coinbase, and Kraken, among others. For this guide, we'll use Binance as an example due to its user-friendly interface and wide range of supported cryptocurrencies.

**Getting Started with Binance:**

a. **Download the Binance App: Start by downloading the Binance mobile** app from the Google Play Store (for Android users) or the Apple App Store (for iOS users). Install the app on your smartphone and launch it.

b. **Create an Account:** If you're new to Binance, you'll need to create an account. Tap on the "Register" or "Sign Up" button to begin the registration process. Enter your email address and create a secure password. Follow the prompts to complete the registration, including verifying your email address.

**c. Secure Your Account:** After creating your account, it's essential to enhance its security. Enable two-factor authentication (2FA) to add an extra layer of protection to your account. You can choose to receive 2FA codes via SMS, email, or authenticator apps like Google Authenticator or Authy.

**d. Complete Identity Verification** (Optional): Depending on your location and the level of services you intend to use on Binance, you may need to complete identity verification (KYC). This typically involves providing personal information and identity documents such as a passport or driver's license.

**e. Fund Your Account:** Before you can cash out, you need to fund your Binance account with cryptocurrency. Tap on the "Wallet" tab in the app and select "Deposit." Choose the cryptocurrency you want to deposit and follow the instructions to generate a deposit address or scan the QR code provided. Transfer the desired amount of cryptocurrency from your external wallet or exchange to your Binance account.

**f. Navigate the Trading Interface:** Familiarize yourself with the Binance trading interface, where you'll execute your cash-out transactions. Explore different trading pairs, order types, and charting tools available on the platform.

**g. Monitoring Your Portfolio**: Once your funds are deposited into your Binance account, you can monitor your portfolio's performance in real-time. Tap on the "Wallet" tab to view your balances and transaction history.

**h. Executing a Cash-Out Transaction**: When you're ready to cash out, navigate to the trading pair corresponding to the cryptocurrency you want to sell. Tap on the "Sell" button and enter the amount of cryptocurrency you wish to sell. Choose a market order for immediate execution at the current market price or a limit order to specify your desired price.

Review the order details and confirm the transaction to execute your cash-out.

**i. Withdrawing Funds to Your Bank Account**:

After selling your cryptocurrency, you can withdraw the proceeds to your linked bank account. Tap on the "Wallet" tab and select "Withdraw." Choose the fiat currency (e.g., USD, EUR) you want to withdraw and enter your bank account details. Follow the prompts to complete the withdrawal process, including any additional verification steps required by Binance.

j. **Confirmation and Transaction** History: Once your withdrawal request is processed, you'll receive a confirmation notification from Binance. You can also track the status of your withdrawal in the transaction history section of the app. Congratulations! You've successfully cashed out your cryptocurrency using the Binance mobile app. Remember to review and adhere to Binance's fee schedule for trading and withdrawal transactions to optimize your cash-out experience.

**Practical**

**Launching into Future Trading on Binance or any other platform:**

**Understanding Futures Trading:** Before diving into futures trading, it's crucial to understand the concept. Futures contracts are agreements to buy or sell assets at a predetermined price on a specified future date. Futures trading allows traders to speculate on the future price movements of assets, including cryptocurrencies, without owning the underlying assets. It involves leveraging borrowed capital (margin) to amplify potential gains or losses.

**Navigate to Futures Trading Section:** Open the Binance mobile app or access the platform on your computer. Look for the section dedicated to futures trading. On Binance, this is typically labeled as "Futures" or "Futures Trading" and can be found in the main menu or navigation bar.

**Account Funding**: Ensure that your account is adequately funded for futures trading. If you haven't already done so, deposit funds into your futures trading account. You can transfer funds from your spot trading account or deposit directly into your futures account, depending on the platform's options.

**Selecting a Trading Pair**: Choose the cryptocurrency futures contract you want to trade. Binance offers a variety of futures contracts, including perpetual contracts and quarterly futures, for popular cryptocurrencies like Bitcoin (BTC), Ethereum (ETH), and others. Select the desired trading pair from the list of available options.

**Choose Trading Type:** Decide whether you want to trade perpetual contracts or quarterly futures. Perpetual contracts have no expiry date and can be held indefinitely, while quarterly futures have fixed expiry dates. Perpetual contracts are popular for short-term trading, while quarterly futures are suitable for longer-term positions.

**Set Leverage**: Leverage allows traders to control larger positions with a smaller amount of capital. Choose your desired leverage level based on your risk tolerance and trading strategy. Be aware that higher leverage amplifies both potential gains and losses, so use leverage cautiously.

**Place Order:** Once you've selected the trading pair, set your desired order type (market, limit, stop-limit, etc.) and enter the quantity of contracts you want to trade. Review the order details, including price, leverage, and order type, before placing the order.

**Risk Management: Implement risk** management strategies to protect your capital and minimize losses. Set stop-loss and take-profit orders to automatically exit positions at predetermined price levels. Calculate your position size based on your risk tolerance and account balance.

**Monitor Your Positions:** Keep a close eye on your futures positions and monitor price movements in real-time. Adjust your stop-loss and take-profit levels as needed based on market conditions and price fluctuations.

**Continuous Learning**: Futures trading requires continuous learning and adaptation to changing market conditions. Stay informed about market news, technical analysis, and trading strategies to improve your trading skills and maximize profitability.

By following these steps and exercising caution, you can launch into futures trading on platforms like Binance and potentially capitalize on market opportunities to generate profits. Remember to start with small positions and gradually increase your trading activity as you gain experience and confidence in futures trading.

## Tradingview

TradingView is indeed a valuable tool for traders, providing advanced charting, technical analysis, and trading ideas. Here's how to integrate TradingView into your trading strategy after registering and funding your Binance account:

**Accessing TradingView:** TradingView is accessible through its website or mobile app. You can log in using your existing credentials or create a new account if you don't have one already.

**Customizing Charts:** Once logged in, customize your charts on TradingView according to your preferences. Choose the cryptocurrency trading pair you want to analyze (e.g., BTC/USDT) and select the desired timeframe (e.g., 1-hour, 4-hour, daily) for your analysis.

**Adding Technical Indicators:** TradingView offers a wide range of technical indicators to enhance your analysis. Experiment with popular indicators such as Moving Averages, Relative Strength Index (RSI), MACD, Bollinger Bands, and Fibonacci retracements. Customize the settings of each indicator to suit your trading strategy.

**Drawing Tools:** Utilize TradingView's drawing tools to identify key support and resistance levels, trendlines, chart patterns, and other visual elements that can help inform your trading decisions. Drawing tools include trendlines, horizontal lines, Fibonacci retracement levels, and shapes.

**Save and Share Ideas:** Save your analysis and trading ideas on TradingView for future reference. You can annotate charts with notes, comments, and labels to document your analysis and trading rationale. Additionally, you can share your ideas with the TradingView community or collaborate with other traders.

**Social Interaction**: Engage with other traders on TradingView by following influential traders, participating in discussions, and sharing insights.

TradingView's social features allow you to learn from experienced traders, exchange ideas, and stay updated on market trends and sentiments.

**Integrating with Binance:** TradingView offers seamless integration with Binance, allowing you to execute trades directly from the TradingView platform. Connect your Binance account to TradingView and access real-time market data and order execution. This integration streamlines your trading workflow and enhances efficiency.

**Backtesting and Strategy Development**: Take advantage of TradingView's backtesting and strategy development capabilities to test and refine your trading strategies. Develop custom indicators, scripts, and trading algorithms using TradingView's Pine Script programming language and backtest them against historical data to assess their performance.

By integrating TradingView into your trading strategy, you gain access to powerful charting tools, technical analysis capabilities, and social interaction features that can enhance your trading experience and improve your decision-making process. Whether you're a beginner or experienced trader, TradingView provides valuable insights and resources to help you succeed in the cryptocurrency markets.

**Here's a step-by-step guide to trading and cashing out using the mentioned criteria:**

**Launch TradingView:**

Open the TradingView platform on your computer or mobile device.

Select the cryptocurrency trading pair you want to analyze (e.g., BTC/USDT) and set the timeframe to the daily chart.

Plot Resistance and Support Levels:

Maxwell Cowell

Identify key resistance and support levels on the

daily chart based on historical price action.

Adjust these levels using the 4-hour chart to

fine-tune your analysis.

Maxwell Cowell

The arrows are pointing at the resistance and support. This is the first thing you have to do on your chart.

Draw Trendlines:

Draw trend lines connecting significant highs and lows on the chart to identify potential trend reversal or continuation patterns.

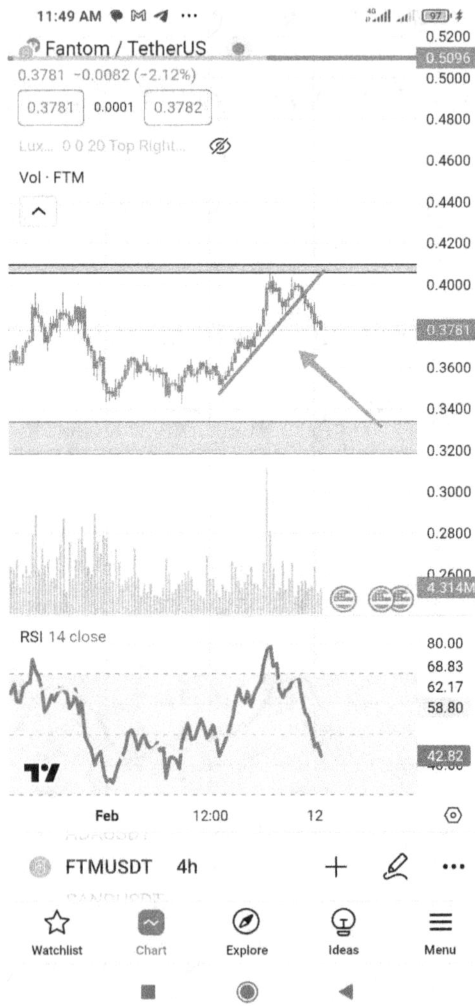



Draw your trend line to touch as many points as possible.

Maxwell Cowell

**Plot Force Volume Graph (FVG):**

Add the Force Volume Graph indicator to your chart to visualize the relationship between price and volume.

Look for divergence or confirmation between price movements and volume to gauge market strength or weakness.

11:49 AM
Fantom / TetherUS
0.3782 −0.0081 (−2.10%)
0.3783   0.0001   0.3784
LuxAlgo - Fair Value Gap 0 0 20 Top Right Small
Vol · FTM
0.4400
0.4200
0.4000
0.3782
0.3600
0.3400
0.3200
0.3000
4.318M
RSI 14 close
80.00
68.83
62.17
58.81
42.91
5          12:00          12
FTMUSDT   4h
Watchlist   Chart   Explore   Ideas   Menu

- **Plot FVG using LuxAlgo fair value gap on trading view.  It automatically prints the gap on your chart.**

**Add RSI and Volume Indicators:**

Include the Relative Strength Index (RSI) and volume indicators on your chart to assess overbought or oversold conditions and confirm price movements.

To plot RSI, go to the indicator section on

tradingview and click on RSI ,it appears

automatically on the chart . Then enable show divergence.

**Conditions to Take a Trade**:

Wait for the price to reach a key level of support or resistance identified on the chart.

Monitor the RSI indicator for overbought or oversold conditions, indicating potential reversals.

Look for chart patterns such as double tops, double bottoms, or head and shoulders formations to signal potential trend reversals.

Wait for a break of the trendline, confirming a shift in market direction.

Pay attention to the formation of the Force Volume

Graph (FVG) and test it at the side where the price

broke the trendline to confirm market momentum.

This picture represents the complete conditions needed to take a trade.

1. Price is at the keyzone ( resistance)

2. There is a spike in the blue volume bar at the keyzone signifying massive pullout of buyers.

3. The RSI is showing overbought.

4. There is the formation of double top.( Price was unable to form a higher high)

5. There is a break of the trend line to the right side ( sell side).

6. There is formation of negative FVG. (Signifying selling momentum).

7. To take the trade wait for the candle to close below the FVG line and opposite candle to

pull back to the FVG.

**Take the Trade:**

Once all conditions are met, wait for the formation

of a confirmation candlestick pattern.

Open the Binance app and navigate to the futures

chart corresponding to the selected cryptocurrency.

Look for a second confirmation, such as an

Exponential Moving Average (EMA) cross on the

futures chart, to validate the trade signal.

Enter the trade when the EMA cross is complete,

confirming the direction of the trend.

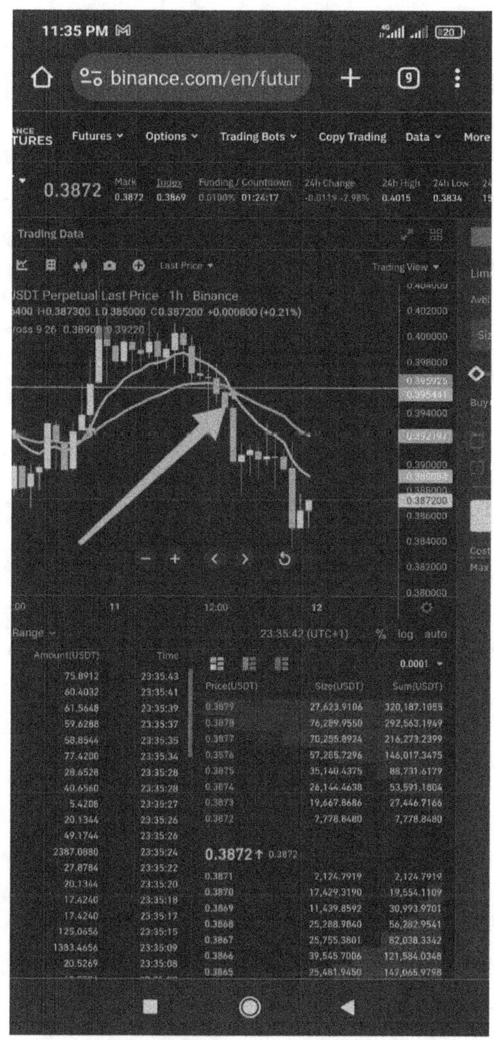

This is the confirmation using EMA cross on

Binance.

Maxwell Cowell

Set Stop Loss and Take Profit Levels:

Place your stop loss order at the bottom of the

double top or head and shoulders pattern, or at a

level that invalidates the trade setup.

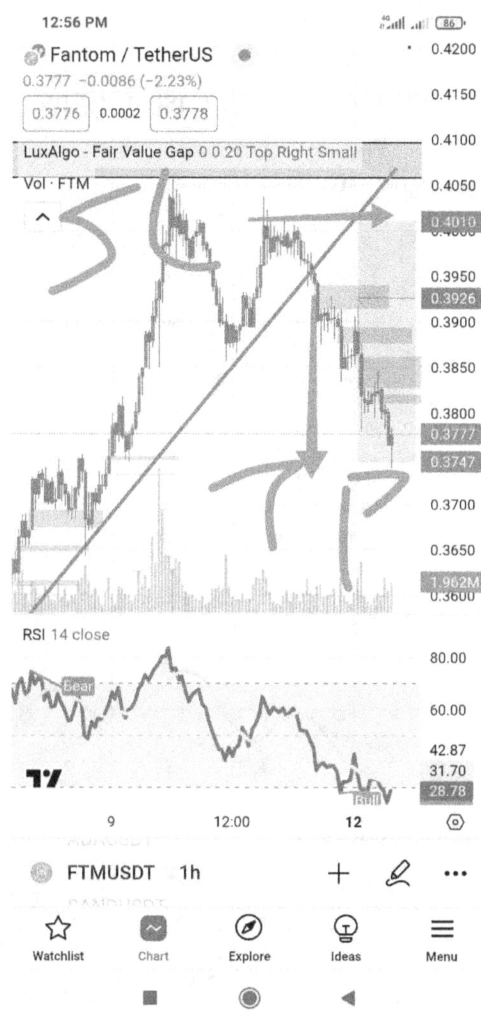


S.L should be placed above the double top

And T.P should be 1:2 or 1: 3

Maxwell Cowell

Calculate your take profit level to achieve a risk-reward ratio of at least 1:2 or 1:3, ensuring that potential profits outweigh potential losses.

Monitor the Trade:

Maxwell Cowell

T.P hit

Maxwell Cowell

Monitor the trade closely, adjusting stop loss and take profit levels as needed based on market conditions and price movements.

Pay attention to any new developments or signals that may impact the trade, and be prepared to exit the position if the trade setup is invalidated.

By following these step-by-step instructions and using the criteria outlined, you can effectively execute trades on TradingView and Binance futures, aiming to cash out profits based on your trading strategy and analysis. Remember to practice proper risk management and continuously monitor the markets for optimal trading decisions.

## Volume

Absolutely, incorporating volume analysis is crucial for understanding market dynamics and confirming potential trading opportunities. Here's how to integrate volume analysis into the trading strategy outlined:

## Plot Volume Indicator:

Add the volume indicator to your chart on TradingView to visualize trading activity accompanying price movements.

Monitor volume bars to assess the intensity of buying or selling pressure during specific price movements.

**Identify Volume Spikes:**

Look for volume spikes or surges in trading volume at key support and resistance levels identified on the chart.

Volume spikes indicate heightened market activity and can serve as confirmation signals for potential trend reversals or continuations.

Interpret Volume Behavior:

Analyze the color and size of volume bars to gauge market sentiment and participant behavior.

A spike in green (buy) volume at a support level suggests strong buying interest and potential bullish reversal.

Conversely, a spike in red (sell) volume at a resistance level indicates increased selling pressure and potential bearish reversal.

Confirming Trade Signals:

Use volume spikes to confirm trade signals generated by other technical indicators or price patterns.

For example, if a double top pattern forms at a resistance level accompanied by a spike in red volume, it strengthens the bearish signal and increases the probability of a successful trade setup.

**Integration with Trading Strategy:**

Incorporate volume analysis into your trading strategy as an additional confirmation tool alongside other indicators and price patterns.

Wait for volume confirmation before entering a trade, ensuring alignment with market sentiment and participant behavior.

**Risk Management:**

Consider volume analysis when setting stop-loss and take-profit levels for trades.

If entering a short trade based on a bearish signal confirmed by a volume spike, place the stop-loss above the recent high and set a take-profit level based on risk-reward ratio considerations.

By incorporating volume analysis into your trading strategy and using volume spikes to confirm trade signals, you can make more informed trading decisions and increase the probability of success. Remember to combine volume analysis with other technical indicators and price patterns for a comprehensive approach to trading the cryptocurrency markets.

**Effective risk management**

Implementing effective risk management and money management strategies is crucial for long-term success in trading. Here's how to integrate these practices into your trading approach:

**Risk Management:**

Set a maximum risk per trade based on your risk tolerance and account size. Many traders adhere to the 1-2% rule, risking no more than 1-2% of their trading capital on any single trade.

Determine your stop-loss level based on technical analysis, support and resistance levels, and market conditions. Place your stop-loss order at a level that aligns with your risk tolerance and trading strategy. Adjust your position size accordingly to ensure that your potential loss, if the stop-loss is hit, remains within your predetermined risk parameters.

**Money Management:**

Once you've entered a trade and the price moves in your favor, consider implementing a trailing stop-loss strategy. This involves adjusting your stop-loss level to lock in profits as the price moves in the desired direction.

When your take-profit level is hit, consider dividing your profits as follows:

Reinvest half of the profits into your futures trading account to compound your gains and increase your trading capital over time.

Divide the remaining half into two portions:

Pay yourself with one portion, transferring it to your bank account or using it for personal expenses.

Reinvest the other portion into your spot trading account to continue building your investment portfolio.

Continuous Evaluation and Adjustment:

Regularly review your trading performance and adjust your risk management and money management strategies as needed.

Monitor the effectiveness of your stop-loss and take-profit levels, trailing stop-loss techniques, and profit allocation methods. Make adjustments based on your evolving trading goals and market conditions.

Maintain Discipline and Consistency:

Stick to your risk management and money management rules consistently, regardless of market fluctuations or emotional impulses.

Avoid over-leveraging or overtrading, as these behaviors can increase the risk of significant losses.

Stay disciplined in following your trading plan and remain patient during periods of market uncertainty or consolidation.

By incorporating robust risk management and money management practices into your trading routine, you can mitigate potential losses, protect your capital, and optimize your long-term profitability. Remember that successful trading is not just about making profits on individual trades but also about preserving capital and managing risk effectively over time.

**Conclusion**:

In the dynamic world of cryptocurrency trading, mastering the art of risk management and money management is paramount to long-term success. Throughout this guide, we've explored various strategies and techniques aimed at optimizing your trading approach and maximizing profitability while minimizing potential losses.

By implementing robust risk management practices, such as setting appropriate stop-loss levels, managing position sizes, and adhering to strict risk parameters, you can protect your trading capital and navigate the inherent volatility of the cryptocurrency markets with confidence.

Similarly, integrating effective money management strategies, such as reinvesting profits, diversifying your investment portfolio, and paying yourself regularly, allows you to grow your trading account steadily and achieve your financial goals over time.

Furthermore, combining technical analysis tools, chart patterns, and market indicators with disciplined risk and money management principles provides a comprehensive framework for making informed trading decisions and capitalizing on market opportunities.

As you continue your trading journey, remember the importance of continuous learning, adaptability, and emotional discipline. Stay informed about market developments, refine your trading strategies based on experience, and maintain a disciplined approach to risk management and money management.

Ultimately, successful trading is not just about making profits on individual trades, but also about preserving capital, managing risk effectively, and achieving consistent, sustainable returns over the long term. By prioritizing risk management and money management in your trading endeavors, you can enhance your chances of success and build a solid foundation for your financial future in the

exciting world of cryptocurrency trading.

www.ingramcontent.com/pod-product-compliance
Lightning Source LLC
Chambersburg PA
CBHW050045260726
48658CB00005B/1785